To Charlie & Laura

Thank you for being Amazing

T. Welson

TIME IS
MONEY

T K WILLIAMS-NELSON

authorHOUSE®

AuthorHouse™ UK
1663 Liberty Drive
Bloomington, IN 47403 USA
www.authorhouse.co.uk
Phone: 0800.197.4150

© *2017 T K Williams-Nelson. All rights reserved.*

No part of this book may be reproduced, stored in a retrieval system, or transmitted by any means without the written permission of the author.

Published by AuthorHouse 03/16/2017

ISBN: 978-1-5246-6648-4 (sc)
ISBN: 978-1-5246-6649-1 (hc)
ISBN: 978-1-5246-6647-7 (e)

Graphic Art by Krishan Shiyani.

Print information available on the last page.

Any people depicted in stock imagery provided by Thinkstock are models, and such images are being used for illustrative purposes only. Certain stock imagery © Thinkstock.

This book is printed on acid-free paper.

Because of the dynamic nature of the Internet, any web addresses or links contained in this book may have changed since publication and may no longer be valid. The views expressed in this work are solely those of the author and do not necessarily reflect the views of the publisher, and the publisher hereby disclaims any responsibility for them.

Introduction

There are thousands of self-development books in the world that aim to provide you with the tools and stepping stones to become successful in body, mind, and spirit. I wanted to be a part of the movement, to help others find their way out from the bottom of the well that many people find themselves in at some point during their lives. Being a *creative* (a shorthand term we use to mean creative *people*) myself, and from such a young age, I've experienced many positives and negatives in the different creative areas that form my life. When I reflect on these experiences now, I realize that I have learnt something from all of them. No matter how small that bit of knowledge was, it helped shape the immense drive that I have today and has inspired me to pen this book.

Time Is Money is a short self-development book for young people, creatives, and people in business. The book is broken down into eight themes and information sections. The themes are made up of my experiences and those of five other young adults in business and as creatives. The themes and information aim to educate, inspire and advise others on different ways to progress forward. We have borne successes, and we have borne pitfalls. We have expressed our inspirations, and we have broken stereotypical representations.

It isn't easy to make that dream a reality as a young person with a dream. Resources and funding are scarce. We apply for job after job only to be told we have no experience, but we can't get experience without a job. *Time Is Money* encourages you to think in original ways and penetrate that bubble known as the comfort zone. All creatives, and people in general, have their highs and lows. Sharing some of those states can inspire others to try something new that can change their life or their perspective on life for the better.

I have been inspired by articles, books, and other content that hasn't always appeared to be positive, but I was still able to take something positive from it. One day when I was working from home, I came across a post on social media about a woman who had lost her son in a tragic accident. But this post wasn't as sad to me as it had been seen by others. She wanted to let the world know that she put some of her son's ashes into a pendant for a necklace so she could have him close to her heart. This one post completely changed my perspective on suffering a bereavement. It highlighted to me that people can find some happiness in their time of grief. The death of her son wasn't the end of her relationship with him; it was the start of a new one. It helped me to understand that something good can always come out of the bad. I have applied that same way of thinking when working towards my goals in life.

It was important for me to include other creatives in this book for two reasons. First, all of us have experienced situations that fit into the eight themes covered in the book. This allows *Time Is Money* to help people who are pursuing different career paths not to be restricted to what I do as an individual. The second reason is that all my creative contributors are people with unique personalities and abilities. I've seen their talents. I've been moved by them all. I wanted them to be involved in the *Time Is Money* movement because they all have a passion. Being passionate about what you do or want to do is meaningful. It will show through what you produce. If you bake a cake but don't like baking, then you won't produce the best cake you are capable of making. Whereas if you have a passion for baking, it should be evident from the time and effort that you invest in your cake. This is a basic analogy, but if you apply it to some of your own situations, it may make more sense to you personally.

My goal for readers is for them to take something away from this short self-development book, whether significant or insignificant, and apply it to their lives in some way. *Time Is Money* discusses ways to make your money stretch further, and to use your time so you have more opportunities to make money. It also reveals external factors of life that can affect you as an individual. Topics such as mental illness, employment, and education are covered in order to keep readers informed on specific areas of health, legalities, and the acquisition of knowledge that concern young people, creatives, and those in business.

This book pushes you to take a risk and see where it goes. But it also highlights pitfalls that you should avoid in different creative industries, difficulties that my contributors and I have experienced, learned from, and now share with the world.

WHO ARE WE?

Tannika K Williams-Nelson

I don't crave attention; I live for respect. That has become a primary motto of mine since becoming the creative I am today. I have always enjoyed reading, writing, and learning – traits that are still embedded in me now and will forever be an important part of my life. Education and creativity are the centre of my world where learning never stops. I take something from everything and anything that I get involved in, be it bad or good. I take pride in everything I do, regardless of what it is, because you never know what could come of it. So why not do it to the best of your ability?

When I attended primary school, I learned how to play the violin and first learned that I am different. I picked up on things fast, and work was never a problem for me, but all I really cared about was sports. It was the same when I moved on to secondary school. I was in the highest class, but even though I loved learning. Sport was my main priority. I was constantly under pressure to exceed expectation in education when what I really wanted was to be an athlete.

Three years into secondary school, our class started final-year exams, and by my final year, my class was given the opportunity to study AS Level English. I acknowledged that I am intelligent and work hard to expand my mind, but I also worked hard at my local track on the weekends and at having an active role in various sports teams at school. It turned out that being an athlete wasn't my true calling, and even though I still continued to train, in my last year of secondary school I self-published my first novel, *Tales of the Hood*.

It was a special moment for me for two reasons. For one, my English teachers had always told me that I had potential to be a writer, especially one teacher, Ms Patel. She had taught me English in my final year, and she gave me the kick-start I needed to begin taking English and writing seriously. She pushed me to my limits, scrutinizing every aspect of my work so I could get better and better at what I did. In the end, it was she who inspired me to start writing a story that turned into a novel, which eventually turned into my first published piece of work. Once *Tales of the Hood* was published, she received the first book that was made, which I signed "To the best teacher ever". It sounds a bit cliché as I'm sure everyone left school with a favourite teacher, but her motivation changed my life for the better.

The second reason why publishing my first novel was so special to me was that I had settled into a talent that could help me progress in many areas of life. Being able to write well about almost anything has allowed me to advise and inspire others as well as to venture out in the world of creative writing.

At the age of 18, I self-published my second novel, *Underclass 7*, which is based on the seven deadly sins. I have always found legends about the seven deadly sins fascinating, and when writing the book, I found the concepts easy to work with in creating a story that even I could become immersed in. I'm attracted to dark dialogue, and have aspirations to write horror and crime books in the future.

I went on to study A levels at Richmond upon Thames College before moving on to study criminology at the University of Westminster in London. In 2015, whilst studying at university, I launched my online fashion boutique, Unique Boutique London, after sketching some fashion designs that I wanted to bring to life eventually as my own creations. I continued writing but took a break from stories and focused on poetry. Also in 2015, I began performing my poetry as spoken word when I attended a local poetry event called Word Up and concluded that spoken word is something I want to be involved with. It is a way for me to express myself indirectly and get things off my chest in a creative and positive way.

When I had to decide what I wanted to do in life, it boiled down to wanting to create something for myself, to building something that I could be proud of that no one could take away from me. From as early as I could remember, I struggled to find a job because I had no experience. But that was a problem with applying for jobs as a first-timer. How were you meant to get experience if no one was willing to give you a job?

When I finally landed my first job at 17, I saw that working for someone else wasn't for me. I was amazed at how badly my fellow colleagues were treated. Yet they didn't feel the need for change. It was as if they were institutionalised. They were so used to being mistreated that they were no longer responsive to it. That was when I told myself that I never wanted to make someone that worked for me feel like that. A happy employee is a productive employee in my eyes. I believe that if you appreciate those who work for you, no matter how menial their job may be, they will reciprocate that appreciation through their work ethic.

I didn't want to work in an environment where it felt like everyone was drowning in a puddle. They had no way to move forward because they had been there for so long, and it would be detrimental to give up the job because they had financial responsibilities. Now that I operate my own business, I can control the way people are treated under my brand. I can assure that people are treated fairly, compensated for their time, and treated in a professional manner because that is the way business should be. Business is all about give and take. You will never be able to do every little thing by yourself, so appreciating those that help me and contribute to my successes is significant to me and always will be.

UNIQUE BOUTIQUE LONDON

Kiraya Kawesa

Kiraya Kawesa is a spoken word poet from London whose plays on words will have you questioning life. At 23 years old, Kiraya has made a compelling break into the world of spoken word poetry, having been inspired by the likes of George the Poet and Sarah Kay. It all started in his first year of university when he wanted to enter a talent show but believed that he had no talent to put out there. After some serious thought, he decided to try his hand at spoken word so penned an inspirational piece called 'Black'. Before performing, his nerves seemed like they were going to get the better of him until he got on stage and gave the best debut performance he could have given. Despite receiving a great response to his performance, it wasn't until Kiraya finished studying at university that he began to take spoken word seriously as a passion.

A main inspiration for Kiraya has been creating a legacy for his family name—something that has been important to him since pursuing poetry. His performance pieces have been inspired by black history and culture, specifically by leaders such as Malcolm X and Muhammad Ali. Reading books was a big part of his development as a spoken word artist, helping him perfect his craft as a writer and learn how to interact with his audiences.

When asked what his performances represent, Kiraya said that they represent him. Every time he goes on stage, it's like speaking to himself in the mirror even though he's performing to a crowd of people. Writing is a way to express his thoughts and feelings to himself first before putting them out to the public.

Kiraya is the first to admit that it hasn't been an easy journey trying to pursue a career path that not many people understand. Being a writer and a performer is about embracing your own identity, and some people may not relate to your identity in the way others do. However, a major highlight of his creative career has been meeting new people at the events that he takes part in and developing new bonds with creatives just like him. It was just by chance that I met Kiraya at my local poetry event given that he lives on the other side of London. But one beauty of poetry and being a creative is that it brings people together unexpectedly. It has been an insightful experience having Kiraya as a creative contributor to *Time Is Money*.

Maverick and Malachi Alfred-Lecky

Brothers and music duo Maverick and Malachi have burst onto the scene in recent years with their creative performance act that fuses together the art of beatboxing with rap. Malachi's lyrical content has been inspired by social and political issues that are present in society today. Together the brothers use their talent to educate and amaze their audiences.

Raised in London, 21-year-old Maverick (real name Reuben) and 18-year-old Malachi have always been an active pair. Both enjoyed sports growing up, including football, basketball, and table tennis, but as they began to understand that music was what they were really passionate about, they turned their attention to busking together – performing in public spaces for voluntary donations – in 2014. Although busking is sometimes considered illegal, resulting in fines and sentences, Maverick and Malachi were determined to let their talent be seen whether people threw opportunities their way or not.

When I worked in Central London, I would see Maverick outside of the tube station on my way to work, beatboxing for crowds that couldn't get enough of what he had to offer. After my shift ended I would head back to the tube station and Maverick would still be there entertaining his audience. I would stand there and admire the dedication that he put in despite being at risk of being removed or worse.

Malachi, who by now had landed a job, would still perform regularly with his brother at various events and festivals to increase their exposure. Maverick became used to performing for the public on the streets. To this day still he embraces every opportunity he can get to showcase his unique craft.

Many musicians seeking to be creatives and putting work out into the world are motivated by profits, but Maverick and Malachi get a thrill out of using their talent to educate others before making a profit for themselves. They want to raise awareness about how to stay true to yourself in a society where conformity is the norm. The topics they cover within their music are deep and thought-provoking, something that seems to be missing from the young generations that will form the future. From teaching people about the capitalism surrounding pharmaceutical companies to motivating people to never give up on their dreams, Maverick and Malachi are inspiring one person at a time with the aim of becoming successful in their music career, having a positive impact wherever possible, and living a comfortable life. Having these two young men involved in *Time Is Money* has been a learning experience. Not all musicians want to go mainstream, and not many male musicians use their craft to tackle sensitive subjects that Maverick and Malachi have no problem working with.

Kimarli Allen

Kimarli Allen is a 21-year-old lyricist and entrepreneur from London who encourages others to expand their minds and explore possibilities. He launched his streetwear brand, ILRAMIK, in 2014 with the slogan 'Bee True Bee You' and since then has done nothing but grow into a conscious person who knows what he wants to achieve in life.

Not only has Kimarli started to build a solid reputation as a businessman, he has already made a significant impact as a rapper who uses his lyrics to express himself and to motivate those around him. His early interests started with music, and even though he was a keen sketch artist and story writer, his aspiration to become a musician and launch his own streetwear brand dominated his life.

Kimarli's inspirations vary, but he has been grateful for the number of opportunities that are available for young people today as a result of the Internet and being able to connect with people in fields similar to his own. Social media has allowed him to interact with his consumers across the globe.

Kimarli studied international business at university as he believes that behind every pursuit there is a business. With the plan set in motion to start his own, he knew that this was the best subject for him in relation to growth and development. I discovered his hidden talent at my local poetry event, and ever since he has been not only a friend, but someone that I can learn from. I've seen him perform often. His captivating personality is constructed around positivity, something that isn't common among young males in our society today. He sets a phenomenal example for young men who want to achieve their dreams despite being surrounded by stereotypes that are more of a hindrance than a help.

Samuel Williams

Samuel Williams is a natural talent. At the age of 24 he has launched his fashion brand, Insane Gentlemen, and has established a successful career in the entertainment industry as an actor, host, and comedian. Samuel's creative spark was evident from primary school, where his acting began, when he took part in a school play and gave a thrilling performance. Samuel went on to study drama at GCSE and A-level.

When he moved on to university, Samuel began to take his acting career seriously. Despite being athletic, with an impressive ability for football, Samuel decided that the creative life is for him. Surprisingly, it was a man selling paintball tickets in 2011 who told Samuel about Starnow, a website that allows you to apply for a range of jobs in the entertainment and fashion industry, including acting jobs. Eight months into his professional acting career, he added host and presenter to his list of talents, and since then he has juggled everything whilst staying on form in each area.

In addition to being an entertainer, Samuel is a wizard with numbers, a skill that can be extremely beneficial for an entrepreneur. He achieved straight A's in mathematics and statistics and has since used his knowledge to get the most out of his money in business and in his hectic lifestyle. Samuel launched his fashion brand, Insane Gentlemen, with clothing made from his own hand-drawn artwork. His unique yet captivating designs form the foundation of what originally was a brand designed for men but was an unexpected hit with women too.

The journey to becoming a successful creative and also a businessman wasn't always an easy one for Samuel. He wasn't always fashion orientated, and had to take the time to learn about how retail and the fashion industry worked before he could think about how his product could stand out from the rest. Forever fuelled by motivation, Samuel did what he had to do, and as a result, Insane Gentlemen was born.

THEMES

Money

Money comes and goes, but what you do with it when it comes is what defines its value. Some people know how to make money, and others know how to make money work for them. Learning the distinction between the two can help you generate more money to fund your dreams. That goes not just go for creatives but for everyone who wants to excel in any field and become financially stable.

Those who know how to make money have no problem working and earning, but the money they earn will go just as soon as it comes, and the cycle will likely continue that way unless they make a significant change. They have no room for flexibility. But those who know how to make money work for them are the ones that seek to get the most value out of their money. Their eggs are never all in just one basket.

For instance, I have worked day jobs that I haven't particularly liked even though my books and my clothing business generate money.

You can never have enough sources of income, and sometimes you will have to do jobs that aren't all that stimulating but allow you to make money that can be directed towards your goals. The more sources of income you have, the more you can make your money work for you.

For example, the income from my day jobs that I didn't like was for me to live on, whilst the money being generated by my other sources of income was directed elsewhere and reinvested into making these other sources of income better. That is how I made my money work for me: directing where my money goes by working out where and how I can get the most value out of it.

Another way that I make my money work for me is by being aware of the media, particularly advertisements. I don't let the media dictate what should be done with my money like a child who see an advert for the latest toy on TV and thinks that she wants it when really she doesn't know what it is but it looks interesting.

It is the same with adults. We spend money using our five senses – sight primarily. Men that like to stay groomed may see an advert for the latest razor set and feel compelled to purchase it despite already having just as good a razor. Similarly, women will see beauty adverts and feel compelled to look as flawless as the models presented before them, so they will spend money to try and achieve that look. We are all unique, and embracing your uniqueness can most definitely save you money. Ladies, you don't have to look like that model on the TV because you are you. There is nothing wrong with wearing make-up, but it is paramount for you to be comfortable in your own skin. Be bold. Be confident because you are beautiful.

Gentlemen, you don't have to splash the cash to impress. Those who are meant to be around you will be impressed not by the way you spend money wildly but by the kind of person you are. It will be your intellect and demeanour that catch the attention you deserve. The point I'm making is that the media, and advertisements in particular, are designed to influence you in what you spend your money on and, in some cases, in your perspective about yourself. This leads on to my next point about living within your means.

Everyone is entitled to spend their money in the ways that they want to, but if you are a young person that has already taken the steps to get into business or pursue a creative career, then the way you spend money will determine how successful you are. What is crucial to remember is that with any new venture, the money doesn't start rolling in straight away. It takes time, patience, and understanding to make sure you have the right resources and mentality to deal with money. Every penny counts.

At first I didn't understand this. Every time I wanted to buy something I would go to the ATM and withdraw money instead of using my card to make the purchase. What I soon began to realize was that when I was withdrawing £10 to make a £7 purchase, that remaining £3 change would always be spent because I physically had it on my person. I would purchase a sweet, not because I really wanted a sweet, but because I knew I had this change in my purse and I might feel for that sweet later. After taking note of this for a while (and wondering why I had so many sweets in my bag that I'd forgotten about), I began using my card to make most of my purchases. At the end of each day, I would transfer all the remaining change from my current account into my savings. Sometimes that would mean up to £9 was going into my savings account every day because the change from those purchases was out of sight, and therefore I wasn't making purchases I didn't need.

This was the first step for me in learning how to budget and get the most out of my money. Hopefully it can be one of many first steps for other young people that want to do the same. In dealing with money, many psychological processes are involved that are different for different people. I analysed and identified mine and found a way to work around them by changing a habit as small as using my card to make purchases rather than cash.

It is easy to get overwhelmed when you have an idea that you would like to bring to life but don't have the funds. You've done all the saving you can and it's still not enough. But there are organisations that can help you if you are serious about what you want to do. Funding and grants are available to help not only young people, but anyone that is trying to pursue a creative career or business venture.

An organisation that is well known for assisting many young people on their way to success is the Prince's Trust, founded by Charles the Prince of Wales. This organisation not only offers advice and training for young people that are unemployed up to the age of 30, they also provide funding and grants for those that have an idea that they want to make a reality.

Arts Council England is another organisation that supports those who want to excel in the area of performing arts. That includes actors, musicians, and other performers that have a passion for what they do and what to take it to the next level. The list of funding organisations that exist is extensive. If you take the time to do your research, you can find an organisation that will want to invest in what you do. There are those that are willing to help young people progress wherever possible. Use these resources to benefit your process of progress.

When you're passionate about what you do, you're more inclined to do it even if it doesn't appear to be profitable to begin with. There is nothing wrong with investing time in improving your craft, which is something both Maverick and Malachi have grown to understand on their journey towards success. Busking has played a significant part in the development of their music careers, and anyone that knows how busking works understands why it is an unpredictable source of income. There is no guaranteed amount of income when you are performing for the public. One day you could make £100 and the next you may only make £20, but when you're passionate about performing, it's possible to look past the money that has or hasn't been made and focus on the exposure that is being gained.

Maverick still takes part in busking, not only as a way of making money to fund further opportunities, but because he loves to beatbox, and people love to see him. On the other hand, Malachi has found security in employment, choosing to work instead of using busking as his main source of income. He still actively performs with his brother at events, spreading his knowledge and positive vibes through his lyrics.

Being able to showcase your talent for free does not mean that you shouldn't know your talent's worth. There are many circumstances where people perform at an event or participate in something for a good cause and therefore have no problem doing what they do free of charge or for a revised fee. In contrast, there are even more circumstances where people can take unfair advantage of you and your talent. At times people will feel that you shouldn't be paid for your craft or the talent that you have to offer. Many times people that I know have expected to get a free book from me because they knew me before I became an author. However, these people take offence when I explain that I have invested time and money into making my novels what they are and that they are worth the cost that they are priced at. This explanation has not earned me any supporters, but I know what my talent is worth, and I know the hard work that went into making my novels the quality material that they are.

No matter what career path you pursue, you will definitely face situations where talking about money and what your talent is worth will be a priority, so it is always good to be prepared to touch upon the subject whether you are requesting a service or providing it.

Money is an essential element of every person's life, and to Kimarli, a business has to be making money in order to be recognised as a business. He believes that if your business isn't generating some form of income, then it isn't really a business. The more money you have, the more options are available to you, which allows you to produce products or provide services of a much higher standard. Money makes a significant contribution to resources, and due to limited resources, Kimarli hasn't been able to produce as many products under his brand, ILRAMIK, as he would like to. However, this hasn't deterred him in any way, and that's what is important when you are setting up a business or have a business set up already. Kimarli has come to realize that the money doesn't always come in straight away, but once it does begin to flow efficiently, then more doors will open and more resources will be available to him in order to grow his business in the ways that he wants to.

Kimarli's thinking about money and his music career is much different from his thinking about money and business. Kimarli says that even though he performs regularly and is always working on new material, the time he dedicates to music isn't motivated primarily by making money, but by getting his name and new brand before the public as a form of promotion. His musical venture is currently built on making the right connections and networking in order to create a project based around music rather than being featured at events and developing music for the sole purpose of generating income.

When you have a clear plan of what you want to achieve, it becomes easier to balance the things you want to do in life. This balance allows you to pursue endeavours that you can monetize while still working on things that you want to do that will take more time and more funding to get off the ground but has the potential to be profitable in the long run.

Many will agree that money is one of the best support systems. Samuel uses money to support his needs and desires. However, he acknowledges that money is only one form of support for someone pursuing a career as a creative or in business. There are various ways to support yourself with a lack of money, for example, using tools such as social media to promote your craft, or by good old-fashioned word of mouth.

Money is often seen as the only thing that can allow you to progress in what you would like to do, but that isn't always the case. Money helps to support your desires but isn't the only way you can make your desires a reality. Samuel came to believe this after once being consumed by materialism himself and learning the hard way that money is to be valued. If you are to make money work for you, it is paramount that you understand the value of it.

Money has played a big role in Samuel's business ventures but has had a limited role in his acting and entertainment career. Samuel used much of his savings to launch Insane Gentlemen. Then he had to put more money into the business in order for it to grow and blossom into what it is today. In contrast, he didn't have to invest much money into pursuing acting. However, the things that he did need to pay for, such as headshots and casting membership fees, were of high quality to ensure that he could attract the best opportunities. He said that acting is based on networking and perseverance – something that will frequently come up throughout this book. He says that unless you are producing your own films or projects, your net worth comes from your network. The same amount of effort that you would invest into a project is the same amount of effort you should invest in creating the best network for what you would like to do. Samuel has also found that budgeting is an important factor when it comes to business, and can be the deciding factor in the success of a business operation.

USE TIME

Being 21 and having accomplished what I have, I get asked a lot of questions when people find out about all the creative and not-so-creative pursuits I'm involved in. The most common question I get asked by nearly everyone I meet is, How do you find the time to do everything? At first I didn't really know. The best way that I could have described it was that I'm on my own little planet when I'm thinking and working towards making myself a better person at everything I do. My brain feels like a computer most of the time, prioritising what is important but never neglecting the details. I'm constantly updating what I need to get completed in my head, so much so that when it's time for sleep, the computer is still fully functioning. The way my mind works helps me to use my time as much as possible, allowing me to stay on top of everything I have to do.

There are twenty-four hours in a day. When we're not sleeping or working, much of the remainder of the day is spent waiting. When I tell people this, it comes across as a confusing statement. However, once I break it down, it becomes more understandable and relatable.

For example, those who, like me, take public transport to get around are usually seen either sitting or standing, waiting to get their destination. That time could be spent planning something or catching up on that new book you've been wanting to get through but can't find the time to read. I never would have been able to write two novels whilst studying if I didn't use my time effectively. I used public transport as an example because I wrote much of both of my novels on the train to and from my studies in addition to working on them at home. If I was taking a bus or train journey, no matter how short or how long it was, my pen and notepad always came with me. I knew that at some point on my journey I'd be able to get something down on paper, and if not on paper, then on my tablet or my phone. Making progress was and still is a process that I didn't want to stop. I knew that I wanted to write books, but I wanted to study and expand my knowledge about crime by studying criminology at university. I had to find a way to make both work for me, and learning how to use my time in this unique way was the starting point for me.

Even though getting the most out of your time is important, it works differently for everyone, depending on your lifestyle and what your talents are. I'll be the first to admit that when my mood isn't the greatest, my ability to use my time effectively decreases. Sometimes I have bad days, and sometimes I have really bad days. Bad days are okay, as long as you can acknowledge that it's only a bad day and does not define your work ethic and your ability to make the most of your time. You'll be ready to pick yourself up and keep moving towards your goal as soon as that bad day passes. It is important not to let a bad day turn into procrastination.

'Procrastination is the thief of time' is a traditional saying that explains in a nutshell why procrastination is detrimental to someone's progress.

It reduces the motivation you have to get things done, and staying motivated is essential to staying balanced on your journey to success.

People procrastinate for various reasons. Sometimes it's because the task that they have to do is something they don't want to do. Therefore they end up doing something else instead or not doing any task at all. Others may not know how to approach the task at hand and choose to avoid it altogether.

An example of this is when people that have read my novels tell me that they would love to write a book. They have noted down ideas and planned out what they want to write about, but don't know where to start. I always encourage these people to just start writing. Don't waste time thinking about *how* you're going to start writing. Just do it. Once you have something down on paper, then you can navigate your story from there.

Not many things come out perfect the first time, no matter how good you may be when you're starting something new, so don't be afraid to make mistakes. Perfectionists also procrastinate because they aren't sure that they will have the time or capacity to complete a task to their high standards. This is a procrastination point that I can relate to. The way I worked around it was by using my time in the ways mentioned above. I like things to be a certain way before I feel happy with them.

This requires me to designate enough time to tasks that are the most important so that they are completed to my high standard. I am the only one that can push the hardest for what I want and where I want to be, and once I eradicated my way of procrastination, I became more productive in everything I did, which felt good – rewarding.

Eliminating procrastination and getting the most out of your time starts with minimising distractions. I prefer to work with some form of background noise. Others find background noise distracting when trying to focus on some tasks. Identify your distractions and identify your own way of minimising them in order to get more done in the time you have allocated to that particular task.

Another tip is to think about how good you will feel once you have complete that task that you've been procrastinating over for the longest time. Like I said above, eradicating my way of procrastination allowed me to become more efficient, and that gave me a rewarding feeling. Find your rewarding feeling after you've completed a task, and use that as motivation to complete another and another.

Finally, for those who find it difficult to approach larger tasks with the same positive attitude as smaller tasks, try breaking that task down into smaller tasks and ticking them off one by one. That way you won't look at the task as too much to handle but easier to handle when broken down to a smaller scale.

These aren't the only ways to combat procrastination and use your time effectively, but these tips can get you started on your way in doing so.

Cutting out the toxic people in your life is also an essential step that will allow you to be more efficient with your time. This doesn't happen overnight, and you will go through some tough experiences along the way when figuring this out.

The removal of negative people from your life is something that Kiraya has found to be a significant step forward in his career. Family and friends that effect the efficiency of his progress and who fail to understand or support his vision have been cut out of his life for the better. In order to make a talent grow, it needs to be taken care of. Part of this process is understanding what is and isn't good for you and investing your time into the *what is* instead of the *what isn't*. If friends or family can't understand why you invest so much time recording your work in the studio yet try to push you in other directions that you know aren't for you, that is a red flag. You know what your passion is, and it's okay if people don't share or understand your passion, but you shouldn't let anyone or anything divert you from that passion if it can be avoided. If that means you have some wrong people in your space, this problem can be avoided or remedied. The more time you dedicate to your craft, the better that craft will become.

I've emphasised that time is of the essence when trying to build a business, and dedicating extensive time to perfecting his craft and covering all angles is the way Kimarli effectively uses his time. From coming up with new ideas and concepts to keeping his social media pages up to date at all times, Kimarli has committed himself to making his brand the best it can be. He gives it all the time it needs to be nurtured, encouraging growth and development and building a platform for the main aim of his brand, which is to inspire others to be themselves and not conform to the norm.

Studying international business at university accounted for a considerable amount of time that Kimarli could have spent focusing on his business. Yet having completed his studies in this field, not only has he learned how to work under pressure, but he has acquired knowledge that can benefit his personal endeavours and his business in both the short and long run.

Using your time doesn't necessarily mean that all your time will be spent on your business or working on your craft. Using your time can involve anything that will help you to excel in the direction you would like to go in. Making the most of the time that you do have to spend on your business or working on your craft is likely to make that direction much clearer for you.

Professionalism

Having a professional attitude and appearance towards what you do or want to do is a catalyst for success. I cannot stress enough the importance of professionalism in business and any other career path that requires you to interact with other people, either directly or indirectly. There have been so many occasions in my life where I have had to let people know that they are unprofessional and that I therefore won't be working with them.

Leaving a legacy in this world means leaving the people you encounter with a lasting impression of you or your brand. For example, when I'm seeking out people to work with in the different creative areas that I'm involved in, I'll approach them via email. Many of these people haven't sent me a response to this day. It takes nothing to reply to someone that is interested in you and your craft, whether it's to say you're not interested or just want to wish someone the best and to network.

Things like this demotivate some people, but the best way to deal with such circumstances is to remain professional and keep working towards your goals. I have learnt that other people's lack of professionalism does not define yours.

Another area of professionalism that may seem obvious but to many people is still not a priority is *organisation*. The more organised you are, the more professional you appear to others. If you are providing a service, that service has to be appealing and delivered properly to the customer.

To promote my fashion boutique, I have collaborated with online media sources that I found to be seriously disorganised. As a result they didn't deliver in the right way the service that I had paid for.

A significant case of this was when I teamed up with an online magazine for some promotional work that included promotion on their social media handles and a video interview that would be done at one of my fashion photo shoots. The social media promotion that they carried out consisted of a few tweets on their Twitter account. Even though I paid for them to promote my boutique on all of their social media handles, they failed to use their Instagram and Facebook accounts, which was the first red flag that they lacked organisation.

If they had a promotion plan for my boutique, then they would have used all their social media accounts with scheduled posts related to my business. The interview with myself had to be rescheduled multiple times due to a lack of communication between the owner of the magazine and their presenter. When the interview finally did happen, it went well, and I started to believe that they were actually following through with what we discussed. We captured behind-the-scenes footage of how Unique Boutique London goes about shooting new arrivals and working with models and the way I like to direct my photo shoots in order to get the results that I want. However, to this day I still have not received the finished product of the interview.

What made the magazine and those involved with it appear even more unprofessional was that the co-owner that I was dealing with got her friend to contact me instead of contacting me herself to let me know that their videographer had run off with my interview footage. Even though I was seeing the same magazine promote interviews that were carried out after mine, they didn't have the decency to work the matter out with me in a professional manner.

Such an attitude is unacceptable in any field of work. Being young does not mean we can use age as an excuse to take shortcuts. Due to this magazine's lack of organisation, they appear unprofessional and are unable to deal with people that are unhappy with the high-standard services they claim to provide. In addition, and probably the biggest let-down of the matter, is that I didn't get value for my money – money that could have been invested into another form of promotion that might have done a better job.

This isn't my only experience that has shown me that organisation is a crucial factor in being professional. Over time you will have your own memorable experiences where you will see how disorganisation can weaken professionalism.

Presentation, presentation, presentation! It is important that you present yourself and your brand in the best way possible. I've already told you about my mistakes with presentation of my debut novel, *Tales of the Hood*. That was enough to teach me that I won't settle for mediocre presentation. However, presentation extends way beyond making something look good. Presentation is your representation of yourself as well as your brand.

Many people that I come into contact with who have visited or shopped on my boutique website comment on how professional it looks, from the range of models used to the consistency in images I use to represent my products. People buy with their eyes. If your website has images that distract from the product you are selling, then consumers won't interact with your website as well as if you had clear, high-quality images of the products you are selling that will appeal to consumers. You need your website, business, or brand to make a good impression in order to leave a lasting impression.

You have probably come across websites that don't look professional and that don't hold your interest. You may assume from their appearance that they are unreliable or that the product you receive won't look like the product you purchased. Whether you are a musician, fashion guru, or a creative, your online and offline presence should be of high priority when aimed at the public. I take pride and invest a lot of time into making my website, blog, and professional social media accounts look presentable because good presentation sells!

Kiraya has had his fair share of experiences with professionalism. Like me, Kiraya views professionalism as a two-way street. In other words, you reap what you sow. In his own words: 'There will be a time when someone will promise you that they will do something for you, and you will expect them to be professional about the matter.' Logically, you would show that same respect in similar circumstances.

As you get older, it becomes clearer that nothing in life comes for free, and I'm not referring just to money. You can't expect to be treated in a certain way if you aren't willing to reciprocate that level of treatment. That is something many young people fail to grasp about being professional. Working with Kiraya on *Time Is Money* stemmed from the exact same thing that this theme has covered: professionalism. I admired his spoken word performance so much at my local poetry event that I wouldn't leave that venue without reaching out to him about featuring him in this book. His professional approach when he talked to me about his craft and inspirations inspired me on the spot. It highlighted to me that there are still like-minded people that know how to represent themselves in the best way.

To Kimarli, professionalism involves using yours skills and talents in a way that represents who you truly are as a person. Many people assume that being a professional means looking smart, speaking immaculate English, and acting a particular way. However, as a young person, being a professional takes on a whole different meaning. "Unreliable", "never punctual", "cracking under pressure" – these are just a few traits that are commonly associated with young people. We are often misunderstood by people who assume that we lack the experience and sheer work ethic to make a valid contribution to business or as a creative.

Stereotypes portray the youth of our society in a negative light, often making us out to be something that we're not. Cases where young people have been unprofessional or violent have been generalised as representative of young people as a whole. Kimarli believes that we as the youth of today have a lot to offer when we are focused and ambitious. Yet that motivation seems to be overlooked when topics such as gun and knife crime dominate the media. Professionalism comes, not with age, but with the desire to make a positive impression among a generation that is regarded with more negativity than positivity.

Learn to evaluate both the things you are good at and the things you know you can improve on. Samuel has learned to do this. He acknowledges that he could improve his professional approach towards others. Samuel has no problem presenting both his brand and himself in a way that stands out. Everything he puts his mind to comes out clean and precise, which is a significant selling point of his brand. You can tell by his setups and displays that he invests a considerable amount of time and money in making sure that Insane Gentlemen is represented in the right way. His business website is simple yet effective, and all these factors contribute to his professionalism.

In contrast, in face-to-face communication, Samuel is sometimes misunderstood in ways that have sometimes been interpreted as confrontational. In reality, he is a man that expresses himself with passion about his business. He has learned that his approach to people can be misinterpreted and has taken steps to work on his interaction with people, observing the situation and adapting when necessary.

Nonetheless, Samuel is great at networking. He understands that networking is a fundamental way to meet new people that can take your business or talent in new directions. It is easy to assume that someone who is direct in his approach to communication is rude or aggressive – which is sometimes true, but in many instances it's not.

I have learnt from openly interacting with the public since publishing my first book that everyone is different. Some people speak in naturally loud voices that can be mistaken for shouting. Others come across as shy and quiet initially, but if you give them a chance, they begin to feel more comfortable and in turn become more talkative. A part of being a professional is understanding that professionalism is a subjective concept that can be interpreted in many different ways.

Sacrifices

A word that many people dread hearing is *sacrifice*. No one, including myself, likes to give up things that they like to do or like to have. However, in order to move forward in life, sometimes you have to see the bigger picture rather than focusing on the sacrifice in the present. Think about how the sacrifice will benefit your progress in the long term. Finding positive justifications for the things you have to sacrifice in order to reach your goals makes you feel better about the sacrifice being made. You're reminding yourself that you desire much more than what you may have to give up for the short term.

My social life after the age of 16 became pretty much non-existent. Once I had gone on to college to study A-level US history, sociology, English, and psychology and wanted to get the best grades that I could, I found no time to have an active social life. And after a while I got used to a routine that revolved around work. I started to believe that I didn't need a social life. The friends that I made in college weren't all that friendly in the long run, and that further reinforced my belief that maybe I was better off focusing all my attention on working towards where I wanted to be. I was quite content travelling to Richmond upon Thames, doing what I needed to do at college, and going home to do more work. The people around me began to see my obsession with work and progression as unhealthy. They didn't understand that I was happy to sacrifice a social life that would most likely comprise partying and spending money that could be invested into an area that would bring me closer to my dreams.

Something that people still tell me is 'You're still young', with the assumption that young people should be living their lives to the fullest and not worrying about serious matters such as setting up a business or thinking about working towards a mortgage. I have a different take on this. Some people assume that young people who are happy to embrace a vigorous work ethic are somehow missing out on life. This is not the case for me. Working towards my goals is me creating the foundations for a better life in the future. I want to travel the world before it's tarnished beyond repair. I want to be able to buy something and not feel like I'm hurting my pocket because I know I can afford it. I want to be able to own my own home. These wants are just a few of the reasons why making my work a priority is beneficial to me.

I do enjoy life, but the way I want to enjoy life at my current age isn't favoured by many of those in my age group. For example, when I have the spare time, I like to go to the museums in London or go to see a show at the theatre. I like to participate in activities that expand my mind in some way, teach me something new, or just inspire me. The people that I'm surrounded by at this time in my life don't see the fun in my kind of social life. They don't seem to understand why I find comfort in going to a museum and taking notes on all the interesting things that I have encountered. They prefer a more active social life—which is fine. I'm not saying I don't like a good night out. Letting your hair down is definitely necessary sometimes, but for me, not all the time.

I usually have work on my mind. I'm always thinking about working on that new chapter when I get home or planning my week meticulously so I make sure I have everything covered. When I have tasks that need to be finished in order for me to progress, I find it difficult to get that off my mind and have fun.

Many of the creatives and business people that I have had the opportunity to meet and interact with have a similar mindset. Others are different. Some people thrive off an active social life, and that is how they make their progress—by knowing and interacting with a lot of people.

Quite a few people in my extended circle love the finer things in life. There is nothing wrong with that if you have an income that allows you to live a lavish lifestyle. Most of those who surround me do not, yet they will continue to live that lifestyle and wonder why they aren't moving forward in the ways that they want to. They aren't investing in moving forward; they are investing in creating an illusion. They are trying to *appear* as if they are moving forward.

When you have a career goal that you would like to achieve that requires money, but you choose to shop the most expensive brands and travel to the most expensive places, then where is the room to make your goal a priority when money is involved? Those who are pushing hard for that goal will be more open to making sacrifices in spending money on wants instead of needs. Money spent on what you want may in the long term be in effect the money you need to get closer to your goal.

I haven't always had this mentality because I have never been much of a big spender. That doesn't mean I don't like nice things. I have made many sacrifices on things I want to buy, places I would like to travel to, and more. However, it was my time at university observing others that made me want to incorporate this theme into *Time Is Money*. I would never forget watching fellow students squander their student loans on designer handbags, clothing, and footwear – money that didn't belong to them. To already have a mentality where you freely spend money that isn't yours is likely to hinder your forward progress due to a lack of discipline.

For example, many young people with good credit have banks contacting them about overdrafts and credit cards. I know I do. However, while some may see these as financial advantages, having credit entices you to spend money that you don't have, such as by going into overdraft for those shoes you've been longing for. *It isn't free money!* Eventually, what you have borrowed must be paid back.

So again, the cycle of working for money and spending it instead of making money work for you comes into play. If you're always paying back because you've overspent, where does investing in your goals come in? Sometimes sacrifices, which can come in many forms, need to be made in the short term to strengthen what is to come in the long term.

People who have immense drive to be the best they can be at what they do in life will understand that at times sacrifices need to be made. Many times Kiraya has had to pass on outings with friends and family or special occasions because he's performing or working on perfecting his craft. People will not always agree with your dedication if it means you have less time on your hands to fit those people in. Sacrifices come in many forms, and in most cases anyone who is working towards a dream will have to make some type of sacrifice. For Kiraya, making sacrifices is all about seeing the bigger picture.

If you have a vision of where you want to be that isn't shared by those around you, then when you make sacrifices, it will be difficult for these people to see the bigger picture and to understand why you made these sacrifices. However, it is for you to understand that you know what the bigger picture is. You know why you are investing so much time, money, effort, and energy into making your dreams a reality. What should make sacrifices worth it is the feeling that you know what you are striving for and that you are willing to do all that you can to move forward.

Similarly, Kimarli has had to distance himself from people that can't understand what he is trying to do and why he is working so hard to achieve it. In addition, Kimarli has had to sacrifice splashing cash on luxuries that he once desired in order to fund projects that he would like to put together and to expand his brand to make it stronger.

Cultivating the ability to identify what sacrifices will be beneficial to you will take time. You may not have to make any sacrifices at first if you are in a good position with what you would like to do, but eventually there will be something or someone that you will feel isn't compatible with your journey, and you will have to make a conscious decision about the approach you will take to dealing with this.

USE TALENTS

Everyone in this world has talents that can change their life. If you read success stories about other people, you often see that in their early lives, they had been investing time in activities such as sport or playing an instrument. As they grew older, it became easier for them to identify which talent yielded the most satisfaction for them, and investing more effort into that talent eventually set them on a course to becoming successful in that pursuit.

Before I started to take writing seriously at the end of secondary school, I wanted to be an athlete. I was a keen sprinter, which my secondary school had acknowledged before I did, and they did everything possible to help me grow as a sprinter during my time there. It was training outside of school that was the problem for me. My parents knew that I loved athletics, but saw it as a mediocre move because I was intelligent. They assumed my intelligence would go to waste if I invested my time and efforts in pursuing a career in athletics. As a result, they never funded any athletics training for me outside of school, and I ended up turning to writing for some form of comfort.

The way I see things now is, if my parents did push me to be an athlete like I wanted initially, then I probably would not have gone on to write two novels and launch my own fashion boutique. Even though being a sprinter yielded the most satisfaction for me at that time, changing my direction and pursuing a career in writing has yielded me satisfaction for the long term. Everything happens for a reason, and when one door closes another one opens, even if it doesn't seem evident immediately. This is why it is important to use any talents you have or to develop the talents that you want to have. You will never know the outcome of something until you've tried it. Life is all about trial and error. If it seems like you're not good at something despite giving it your all, then try something different. In the process of trying something different, you might find ways to help you progress in your first venture.

I've been working towards a creative career although I was a devout academic up until leaving university in 2016. However, I have always loved studying and learning new things. I studied US history and British history in college, which has inspired many book ideas for me. I graduated with a bachelors degree in criminology from the University of Westminster in London with a plan to use much of what I have learnt in my future writings. Writing, designing, and business are the pursuits I want to follow in life. I understand that expanding my knowledge and using that knowledge in the areas I want to excel in will make what I produce much better.

People ask me why I went to university to study criminology. I say because I want to write crime books. That was the initial reason why I went on to study this subject. I wanted to learn about the fundamentals of crime and the legal system so I could produce quality crime books with an urban twist. No one could understand why I would do such a thing, but that didn't matter. Now that I have graduated from university, not only do I have the quality knowledge to produce the crime books that I want to write, I have also expanded my knowledge on how to apply the law to different areas of my life. For example, I know my employment rights, so when issues have arisen in the workplace I have used this knowledge to make my case. Similarly, I've had business disputes that have been resolved because I know the relevant business law associated with my business. Therefore, by going to university to learn about crime, I was able to use the knowledge I acquired and use it to benefit my other areas of work and talent.

A talent that I didn't know I had but now love and embrace is baking. It surprised me when I woke up one day and told myself that I wanted to learn how to bake cupcakes. It was that easy to get into something new: Wake up and believe in it!

Around the time this thought came to mind, I was thinking about planning a pop-up shop event for my fashion boutique and was brainstorming ways that I can make the event more than just a pop-up shop. In order to keep the costs of the event as low as possible without compromising on quality, I wanted to do things for myself instead of purchasing the services of others. Baking cupcakes was one of them. I had no idea where to start, so I did what I always do when I need some visual inspiration: I searched how to make cupcakes on YouTube, a brilliant source for inspiration on anything and everything.

It wasn't baking the cupcakes that worried me when I made up my mind to take on this new challenge and develop a new talent. The problem was the icing. It was difficult to get the consistency right at first. Then when I jumped that hurdle, the next obstacle was creating a decorative cupcake that would be appealing to the eye. I watched video after video, purchased baking books, and baked continuously until I got it right, as I knew I would. It was a talent that I wanted, and I put in the work for it. In less that two months, I had mastered how to bake flavoured cupcakes with melt-in-your-mouth icing that were worthy of selling. I cultivated this new talent for myself, and now I can use it for events, gifts, and much more.

Anything I put my mind to doing, I give it 100 per cent every time and take pride in everything I do, even if it's something that's not necessarily pleasant. That is a talent in itself – knowing your capabilities and always trying to make them better. Talents can be created, altered, and mastered if you put your mind to it, and anyone who wants it enough will find a way to make it work. Wake up one day and tell yourself you're going to try something new, then stick to it!

For some people, discovering that they have a talent may be the angle that they find the most difficult when considering what life choices to pursue. From Kiraya's perspective, all talent starts with self-belief. When he first started out in poetry and began performing his work, Kiraya didn't believe that he was good at what he did. Even after he came across as a good performer to audiences, his lack of self-belief hindered his progression to be a great performer. His lack of self-belief meant that he wasn't being the best he could be when he stepped out on stage. Not until Kiraya believed in what he was doing, understood that he had a passion that he wanted to share with the world, and identified that he wanted his words to inspire and help others did his true talent emerge.

That raw talent inspired me to feature him in *Time Is Money* after seeing him in his element. In contrast, Kiraya has found that self-assessment is just as important as self-belief. In his eyes, self-assessment is key to the growth of artists. Without it, it is easy to become repetitive and uninspired because our strengths and weaknesses are unclear to us. As a result, it becomes more difficult to progress because we are unaware of what we could do better and how.

Throughout this book, I have tried to emphasize the idea that inspiration can come from anywhere at any time in any form. Maverick and Malachi are no different when it comes to being inspired to use their talents to create something memorable. Maverick started to beatbox from a young age. As Malachi became more socially aware, he became even better with words. However, it was their parents who encouraged the two of them to fuse their talents together. Using your talents doesn't mean taking from every little thing you may be good at, but being able to adapt and adjust talents, however small, so that they complement the other areas of your work that are a priority.

Malachi could have pursued a conventional career in music but has seen that his craft is better and, more importantly, unique when combined with Maverick's beatboxing expertise.

THE MEDIA

The media as an institution has the ability to influence the public's perspective on life. In my encounters with the media there have been both positive and negative outcomes. These have shaped my views about the society I live in as well as the world as a whole.

One important encounter I had with the media was related to the release of my first novel, *Tales of the Hood*. I began writing it at the age of fifteen when I was still in secondary school. I had always been good at English, and in my final year, my English teacher inspired me to write more because she believed I had talent. I took her advice and started to brainstorm some ideas, but nothing stuck with me.

Not long after I began to take writing seriously, a wave of youth violence swept through London. What became known as *postcode wars*, made up of meaningless violence between groups of boys and young men from different areas, had people fearfully avoiding certain places. Boys and young men weren't safe, neither those who were perpetrators of this type of violence nor their victims. It was an unpredictable time for youth culture in the less privileged areas of London. Even at that age I could see that. Innocent people would get caught up in these random violent breakouts.

Meanwhile, the media wasted no time reporting on the dysfunction that was occurring. Newspaper headlines solidified stereotypes that are still trying to be broken today, and the media in general represented young people as a problem without a cause.

The fact that we as young people didn't have a voice or a platform to talk about what was happening from our side of the fence gave me the urge to write about what was going on around me and the sights that I had seen. It was always terrible to hear that another youth had been killed or seriously wounded by other youths that lived literally minutes away from each other. However, I sensed that a story needed to be told from a youth's perspective – from *my* perspective. After all, the violence was happening within the youth subculture, and at the time I believed that it must have been difficult for older generations to understand why this was happening in our society.

I loved writing fiction, and I wanted to incorporate my views and experiences in a fictional novel centred around gang violence and youth culture in London. I self-published *Tales of the Hood* for the first time eleven months later. When the book first came out and I began to promote it, I received a lot of media interest, which was both overwhelming and exciting at the same time. I was interviewed by local media, and at first everything seemed great. People were surprised but impressed that I had chosen to write a book based on such a topic at such a young age.

The media was interested in *Tales of the Hood* until I made it clear that I wasn't involved in a gang myself, but that truths about what happens on the roads with young people is woven into this fictional novel. It became evident that the media was interested in *Tales of the Hood* only because they assumed that I was involved in the criminal activities and processes described in my novel. More people would have taken notice of *Tales of the Hood* if I had been a gang member myself or a female associated with a gang who penned a book after changing for the better. They failed to see that a young, black female can see what is going on in society for herself and write her story. It was an odd ordeal, being so young and unable to understand why it would have been better if I had been bad.

As I grew older, became more educated, and studied the media, I realized that two dynamics were at play concerning the media's reaction to my first book. The first was *novelty*. The novelty of a story is what makes it more newsworthy. A young female who has written a book isn't considered particularly newsworthy, but a young female who has been involved in gang activity and the negative aspects of youth culture writing a book on the horrors she has seen and experienced during this time would have made a better news story.

The second dynamic at work was *race*. Gang violence in London is predominantly associated with black males and with a police force called Trident that is dedicated to combatting gang violence within the black community. The media assumed that I, being a young, black female, would have had some active involvement in the activities described in my novel. If a young Caucasian female had written a book based on gang violence and youth culture in London, the media would have exhibited a much different reaction. They wouldn't be asking her if she was associated with gangs and gang violence. They would praise her for raising awareness about a social issue that is plaguing the city and is commonly associated with the black community.

Race will always play a part in the way people are represented by the media. This insight was an important influence on me when I was working on this book. *Time Is Money* has given me a platform to represent young people as positive, ambitious, and driven persons that are capable of making a good impact on others around them.

One way that I have learnt to get the best results from the media is to approach them from all angles. In reality, not everyone will be interested in what you have to say – but *someone* will be. People may be classified by many characteristics. The media targets them by category. For example, when I promoted my second novel, *Underclass 7*, much of the general media paid little interest, but being a young, black female from London meant that I could contact media that focused on young people and youth culture. I was able to contact media outlets that had female and ethnic minority audiences, which led to me being featured in *The Voice* newspaper. I also got in touch with local media outlets that jump at the chance to write something positive about parts of London that are categorised by social deprivation.

It took me a while to realize that there are many ways to generate media attention. It starts with looking at yourself as an individual. It requires breaking down your persona, starting with your physical appearance and attributes, and progressing all the way to your interests and inspirations. Not all media is bad, and in many cases the media is a beneficial tool if handled with care.

The point that I'm highlighting here is to stay true to who you are when dealing with the media. I could have easily embraced the attention for all the wrong reasons. I could have said, Yes, I have been involved in the activities that are featured in my book, when I haven't – just to get ahead, just to give the media what they wanted, and just to make more money. The media has advantages and disadvantages. It's good be aware of the differences in the way the media report on various topics.

My earlier example was about race, but here I'm referring to the difference between tabloid newspapers and broadsheet newspapers. Many people are unaware that tabloid newspapers, such as *The Sun* and *The Daily Mail*, are likely to report stories that are considered the most 'newsworthy' – content that can easily be sensationalised to make the story more popular and readable for their target audiences. On the other hand, Britain's most popular broadsheet newspaper, *The Daily Telegraph*, is more likely to report stories that have a more substantive basis and that appeal to a more intellectual audience. Broadsheet newspapers tend to use a formal tone in comparison to tabloid newspapers, which tend to use an informal tone. Tabloid newspapers are typically associated with working-class audiences whereas broadsheet newspapers are typically associated with middle- and upper-class audiences.

These differences, however small or big, can influence the way you feed your mind and what you make of the society that surrounds you. It would be an understatement to say that the media is an effective tool, but it's up to you to determine how effective a tool it is by doing your research and identifying what media representation would best suit you. Take the time to look at both local media outlets and national media outlets because every bit of promotion for your brand or craft can help you move closer towards where you want to be.

It would be odd to have a theme covering the media that pays no attention to the rapidly growing phenomenon of social media. Social media is one of the most effective forms of free marketing. It can enable you to get your brand, business, or talent seen and heard by thousands. It is definitely a tool that everyone who is pursuing a creative career should have.

Be aware, though, that you have to be smart when using social media to represent yourself professionally. The most crucial thing to do when representing your brand or business on social media is to separate your personal accounts from your business accounts. This is something I have done from day one, since using social media for my books and business, and it is a piece of advice that I urge all young entrepreneurs to take. Content that you would post on personal social media accounts might be unsuitable if posted on accounts that represent your brand or business. For example, if you have a graphic design business, but are continually posting videos of your nights out with friends and content that has no relevance at all to your business, this content will distract audiences from focusing on your graphic design work if they are more interested in what you got up to on Saturday night. By no means am I saying that you can't have fun on social media and express yourself the way that you want to. But just as there is a time and a place to say things in the real world, there is in the virtual world, too. You don't want to give other professionals, customers, and potential customers the wrong impression of you when they visit your professional social media pages.

Another thing to take note of when using social media is to be careful what you say and how you say it, paying particular attention to sensitive issues. When I tell people this, they immediately think of freedom of speech and assume that this means that they can say whatever they want.

If you are pursuing a career in any industry or have a significant influence your industry already, then social media can be a shark tank if you voice opinions that go against the majority. Certain things you say may come back around to haunt you in future.

A case of this involved female rapper Azealia Banks, who is known for publicly criticising the music industry for cultural appropriation by Caucasian musicians who 'feed off' black culture. Yet she voiced some strong racist views on social media towards former member of One Direction, Zayn Malik, using degrading insults such as 'punjab' and 'paki'. When I saw this, I was disappointed that another female from an ethnic minority background could be so immature to use race as a verbal weapon. It also highlighted to me that it doesn't matter if you're in a position of influence like a celebrity. You will still be penalised for expressing inappropriate views. Bank's twitter account was suspended, and she received heavy backlash from not only her fans, but from others who understood that her behaviour was wrong and shouldn't be allowed to go uncensored. She has now portrayed herself to the world through social media as someone that is in favour of discrimination when it suits them, but also has a problem with discrimination if it concerns black people.

I've highlighted both the negatives and the positives that I have faced with the media, but everyone has a different take on this influential institution. Kiraya believes that the media allows artists to remain independent instead of focusing on being signed. It is no secret that social media is a massive platform that encourages artists to promote themselves and release their music, poetry, or other content without being controlled from behind the scenes.

The media has been a great way for Kiraya to find people that support what he does and what he wishes to continue doing for a living. He has made use of the media to support his craft by uploading content on platforms such as YouTube and to Soundcloud, which connects people together using visuals and audio, often increasing their reach and maximising their audience. Free media platforms that allow you to share, subscribe, and meet like-minded people can make a major difference to your progress if you lack funding to pay for more extensive forms of promotion.

In contrast, Maverick and Malachi are artists, too, but have a different view on how social media plays a role in people's lives. The brothers use social media to share their talent with the world, but both agree that social media and the media in general can be helpful only if you know what to do with it. It is a commonly known fact that the media can be manipulative. Maverick believes that the media allows people to detach themselves from who they really are. People can become consumed by materialism and eventually by the media itself. Social media controls people's lives without them even knowing it.

For example, many people document every detail of their lives on social media platforms. The development and easy access to applications that allow communication and interaction has blurred the lines between what is considered appropriate to broadcast to the world and what isn't. The media provide Maverick and Malachi as musicians with a platform to share their work with no boundaries, but they have created boundaries of their own in order to make the media work for them.

Samuel takes full advantage of the media in his career. Being an entertainer for a living, he has a personality that makes him easy to interact with. With over three million views on his Vine comedy videos and hundreds of positive comments, it's no wonder why Samuel is such a good person to have as a contact and friend. He regularly conducts interviews with other creatives and artists, giving them exposure and genuinely taking an interest in what other young people are doing in life.

Samuel's approach to using the media is one reason why he sets such a good example for other young people in our society, especially young men. He has highlighted that despite having his own brand and a rapidly developing entertainment career, he still takes the time out to give back in some way. He takes the time to learn something new even if that something new isn't helping him move forward in his own venture but is supporting someone else's. Samuel's attitude towards using the media demonstrates how the media can be used beneficially when creating audio content through his podcasts, and how social media handles can build bridges between customers and retailers across the United Kingdom.

In addition to the way he makes the media work for him, Samuel has had nothing but good experiences with the media representing him as the entrepreneur he is. He has had successful radio and video interviews for Insane Gentlemen as a result of networking at various pop-up shops. More importantly, he hasn't received any negative feedback from the media. It is easy for the media to manipulate things to support their own agenda, but there is nothing to manipulate here. Samuel is the real deal. By hard work and dedication, he has established a lifestyle that other young black men can aspire to and build upon.

Pace Yourself

Pacing yourself at what you do keeps the mind prepared to take on new challenges and avoid the feeling of being overwhelmed by all you may have to do. I learnt this the hard way when I went about self-publishing my first novel, *Tales of the Hood*. I had written a complete book about something that meant a lot to me, but I was barely 16 and was soon to encounter many problems. I was excited and I was nervous, but I couldn't wait to get my manuscript published for people to read. I had done my research on both traditional publishing and self-publishing options, and I came to the conclusion that my odds were against me if I went down the traditional publishing route. The works that the majority of the traditional publishing houses were publishing at that time were written by middle-class Caucasian authors who covered more traditional genres such as romance, thrillers, and mystery.

My novel was as urban as you could get. Even though the main body of my novel was written in English, much of my dialogue was made up of slang terminology that was used at the time I wrote the novel. My novel also covered sensitive issues such as male rape and suicide despite it being a fictional story. It was a novel that didn't fit in with the sort of novels that traditional publishing houses appeared to be interested in, so I turned my attention to self-publishing.

My problems emerged as a result of not doing enough research into self-publishing, neglecting to pay attention to the differences between self-publishing in the United Kingdom and self-publishing with companies abroad. The result of this was that I eventually self-published my debut novel with an American company. I took everything that this company had told me at face value, all because the only thing that was really on my mind was getting people to read this story I had penned and truly believed was great. I didn't pace myself, nor did I ask the questions that I should have. And they didn't give me all the information that I should have been told to make my book the best it could have been before being available to the public. They had created an amazing front cover for me that I instantly fell in love with, which further contributed to my eagerness.

By the end of the self-publishing process, I was really happy with how things were coming along. The book received a considerable amount of media attention from outlets such as the BBC, various newspapers and other print media, and online sources. It was not until I got the chance to sit down and read over my story again in its book form that I realized that the text had not been edited and formatted correctly. It was a devastating blow to what I had considered the highlight of my life so far. Even though no one cared that there were some spelling errors in the book and that it wasn't formatted in the way that a book should be formatted, it was a big deal for me. This was my story – my product, and I wanted it to be perfect. But I didn't pace myself and take the time to understand the self-publishing process.

This was a major revelation for me, and ever since that experience, I found that you can never do enough research. You can never know enough about what you want to. When you think you know enough, dig even deeper and find that one thing you still don't know. It is this approach that I apply to everything I do now, and is an approach that I would recommend that all people use when looking into something new to make sure you have covered all angles concerning what you need to know.

Among young people is a dominant notion that health isn't all that important at our age. We're not getting unnecessary aches and pains.

We can run for a bus if we need to, and we can handle stressful workloads, but we're still human. Taking on too much can do mental and physical damage. I know how it feels to become overwhelmed from doing too much and when everything seems to be going wrong. It has taken me time to understand that I need to take a break sometimes even if I don't want to.

Some people don't deal easily with pressure. I have seen pressure make people crumble. Young people and mental health have a long history together. Sometimes working so hard because you want so badly to reach your goals can trigger mental health problems such as depression and anxiety.

Young Minds is an organisation that provides advice, support, and information on mental disorders that affect young people. Their primary aim is to empower and embrace children and young people through emotional well-being. It is a great resource for young people who feel like they are struggling with the pressure of striving for greatness. It isn't bad in any way, shape, or form to ask for help. You will produce the best only if you keep your mental balance at its best. Getting things off your chest is one way to stay on track. Yes, we want to be successful, but not at the expense of our mental and physical health. We need to pace ourselves in life in order to be the best that we can be. There is more information on organisations that deal with mental health and statistics towards the end of this book.

Pacing yourself applies not only to when you're working but also to looking after the way your body is working. Kiraya found this out the hard way when one day, after not getting enough sleep for six months straight, he couldn't take it any more. His body completely shut down, and he began shaking uncontrollably. The pressure of sleeping four hours a night to get up and go to work in the morning then perform in the evening became too much, and Kiraya was forced to take a break from his hectic lifestyle. Eventually his body began to stabilise, and he fell asleep. He woke up over ten hours later feeling refreshed and very much relieved that his close encounter did not turned out to be much more serious.

The experience has taught Kiraya that working towards your goals will always be important, but looking after yourself while you're working towards these goals is just as important. When you pace yourself, you allow yourself time for preparation and therefore can create a schedule that isn't gruelling but allows you to get everything done in a healthy and productive way.

It is common for people to say that men are unable to multitask, but Samuel takes multitasking to a whole new level, a level that can be both beneficial and detrimental. Being a creative in the fashion industry takes a lot of work, especially when you have an active role in the creative process of your products. Samuel not only runs his fashion brand but has an active acting and comedy career that is rapidly taking off.

At one stage, he had to work on filming for a movie during the same period in which he had his popular pop-up shop set up at the Bluewater shopping centre in Kent. After filming in the early hours of the morning and for the first part of the day, he had to immediately set out to his pop-up shop space in Kent a fair distance away. This was a routine that he had to keep up with for almost two weeks straight.

On the surface, Samuel appeared to be killing two birds with one stone and reaping the benefits of both worlds. However, the fast-paced approach is not always the best approach, and sooner or later your body will need time to rest and recover in order to function efficiently. In this case, Samuel handled the pressure and workload well as a result of being organised. He had to work out the best way to achieve what he had already committed to without burning himself out in the process.

That isn't an easy task for anyone. It is crucial that you pace yourself when pursuing your endeavours. Always have enough in the tank to capitalise on an opportunity wherever it may come from. Your brain needs to be looked after in order for it to look after you.

Energy

Something that I have found helpful on my creative and business journey is understanding that there are different energies all around us. When I say *energy*, I'm referring to the space around you and the people in that space.

Since I spend much of my spare time alone, I am receptive to the energies of other people. Observation is key for me. By observing body language and listening to the way people talk and the things that they talk about, I've learnt how to read between the lines. I can sense whether a person has an energy that isn't compatible with my own. In turn I can start to think about the type of connection, if any, that this person and I can establish.

People that aren't supportive of what you do, be it friends or family, people who always find ways to highlight your shortfalls without giving constructive criticisms, are ones who have a negative energy that isn't compatible with your own. Instead of understanding that you are pursuing your own goals and finding ways that are best for you to do this, they prefer to look at what you're not doing. This negative energy can begin to affect you and your perspective. You may start thinking that you're not good enough or that you should do things in ways you aren't comfortable with to please others.

You will always encounter people who will put you down and want to see you fail. Some will show this in obvious ways, and others more indirectly through the things they say or the way that they act. Only you can do something about the energies that surround you and identify how these energies can impact you and your craft.

Negative energy can also affect your work ethic. If you are in an occupation that makes you unhappy, yet that is where you spend most of your time, you could become consumed by negative energy that slowly manifests itself as a negative thought process.

This was the case for me when I worked in retail. It wasn't a stimulating environment for my mind, and having to deal with customers' verbal abuse and impatience day in and day out started to take a toll on my outlook on life. I started to think that I wasn't going to progress if I stayed in such a negative environment. And if there was no room for progression, then where was I going to end up? It got to the stage that even before I left my home each day, I was already dreading going to work because it was filled with negative energy.

No one was happy, including me, and it was this that encouraged me to make a change. I had to get out of that environment, but I also needed to find what I really wanted to do in life. In the end it came down to limiting the negative energy that was in my life and replacing it with more positive energy. Negative energy will always be out there, but you need to find a balance.

I reduced my hours at work so that I was still earning an income but spent less time in the negative environment. I replaced my retail work hours with creative work that gave me a positive feeling: I wrote new poetry or worked on new fashion designs. As soon as I made this change, people noticed that I was happier with what I was doing in life and where I was heading. I didn't feel so glum going to work any more because most of my energy was being invested into my creative pursuits – activities that I was passionate about.

It is essential that you surround yourself with positivity wherever possible, regardless of what career path you want to follow. My favourite event that I attend regularly because of the positive energy that fills the atmosphere is my local poetry event, Word Up. Created by husband and wife, Charlie and Laura de Courcy, Word Up has allowed both established poets and new poets to express their talent in a space where they won't be judged but will be embraced by all who watch their performances. You always leave the Word Up feeling exhilarated because you're taking all that positive energy home with you. That energy manifests itself as motivation – motivation to start writing poetry or to find other events that will give you a similar feeling or stimulate you to become creative in a way that suits you.

Work on what type of energy you want your life to be built on. If you want success, surround yourself with ambitious and successful people that you can learn from on your journey. Don't fall out with everyone that doesn't do the same things as you or with those who don't do things in the same way you like to do things. It is often difficult to differentiate negative people from people who are simply going in a different direction from you. That doesn't mean that you can't learn something different from these people who are just as ambitious but chasing a different dream.

Be selective about who you allow into your space. However, you should also learn when to accept some people who can be valuable companions for their support and knowledge. They may teach you something new or make you see things from a different perspective. The positive opportunities that can arise from being around the right people are endless.

In contrast, Kimarli has expressed that if you sit around people who have nothing but bad vibes towards you and who feel comfortable watching from the sidelines instead of getting in the game, then it will be harder for you to maintain your own place in the game. The dead energy carried by negative people around you is contagious and can cause you to overlook positive opportunities as a result of being weighed down by this negative energy.

YOUNG PEOPLE AND MENTAL ILLNESS

The subject of mental illness is broad and has been widely discussed for decades. In particular, much research and development has been made in the area of young people and mental illness that has aided me on my journey to being the entrepreneur I am today.

One thing that I have always admired about myself is my ability to narrow my focus and work hard to achieve what I'm striving for. As I grew older, my way of working hard started to become unhealthy. When I was studying, I had to do well. It wasn't an option for me to fail. That is what I used to remind myself every time I felt demotivated. Initially, I saw this as a beneficial way of thinking because it kept me on my toes. I started college with high expectations for myself because I was used to being good at everything I put my mind to.

But it got to the stage where working was all I was doing. I would spend days on end following the same routine: wake up, get dressed, eat, work, and go to bed. I stopped going out with the few friends that I had. Revising for exams whilst working on my second book was all I cared about. My parents became concerned even though I felt fine. To put their minds at ease, I began spending more time working outside of the home at libraries. To me, this mentality and attitude of dedicating all my time to working on my goals meant that my goals were being ticked off and I was making the progress that I needed to make. To those on the outside looking in, I had completely shut myself off from the world. I wasn't living; I was existing. I didn't want to be social, I just wanted to stay focused and do what needed to be done.

This way of thinking followed me up until university, and it was only then that I realized that I had become an introvert. I wasn't comfortable being around a lot of people for extended periods of time. My university life was made up of working to meet my deadlines at least two weeks early so I could juggle my studies, run my fashion business, and work part-time. I didn't chase the typical university experience that most of the students around me were so excited about. I attended two university functions in my three years studying criminology, and I had no problem with that. But people around me started to have a problem with it. Therefore I soon found myself wanting to be completely alone so that I didn't have to hear it any more.

Eventually I was encouraged to get involved with cognitive behavioural therapy (CBT), in which I had to meet up with a therapist once a week and take steps towards challenging my thought process. At first I didn't want to be there. I didn't want to talk about anything that was on my mind because I was used to dealing with my issues on my own. You think to yourself, *Why am I going to sit here talking about my life to a stranger?* Especially when you're asked to address things you would rather forget. But for the sake of my parents, and to some extent myself, I gave it a go. I was asked to think about why I liked to work so much. What was it about working and being away from people that made me feel so comfortable and secure?

After a few sessions it became evident that I was using my work to avoid interaction with people. I didn't want to form attachments with the unexpected. But with work, I always knew what the outcome would be because of how much effort I put it. I knew I was intelligent and hungry for a better life. These were traits that no one could take away from me, but relationships, friendships, and even family bonds always ended up fading out. That was what made me feel so comfortable and secure about dedicating practically every waking moment to grafting towards what I wanted achieve.

CBT has helped me to analyse my thoughts on a deeper level than I did before I began the process, and to understand that mental illness can come in many forms. In my case, I suffered from social anxiety, but I found something that worked for me and have been able to manage my anxiety in my own way. I have become interested in meditation and yoga. As a result of working in fashion and being an author, I'm always around people and have come to enjoy being in a positive atmosphere with others. I have grown to love networking and meeting new people that I can establish working relationships with.

What CBT has taught me is that I can still dedicate all my time and energy to work, but I need to do this in a healthy way. I have learnt how to take pride in my work by being more open about what I do and why I do it. Not everyone is as lucky as me. Many young people struggle with mental illness daily, unaware that organisations and resources exist that can help them. The stigma of what someone with mental illness is thought to look and act like has made persons who suffer from mental illness afraid to speak up. Even I, as strong and determined as I am, have needed to take the time out of my hectic lifestyle to nurture myself inside and out. Suffering in silence is not the way to heal the mind, body, and soul.

STATISTICS

- In the UK, suicide is the biggest killer of young people, both male and female, under the age of 35. In 2014, 597 young people between the ages of 10 and 24 committed suicide. A total of 1,556 young people under the age of 35 took their own lives in 2014, amounting to approximately 4 people per day. (Papyrus, 2016).

- In 2013, 6,333 suicides were recorded in the UK for people aged 15 and older. Of these, 78 per cent were male, 22 per cent were female (Bromley et al., 2014).

- In 2003, 20 per cent of adolescents may experience a mental health problem in any given year (WHO, 2003).

- In 2005, 50 per cent of mental health problems are established by age 14 and 75 per cent by age 24 (Kessler et al., 2005).

- In 2013, there were 8.2 million cases of anxiety in the UK (Fineberg et al., 2013).

- In England, women are more likely than men to have a common mental health problem (McManus et al., 2016) and are almost twice as likely to be diagnosed with anxiety disorders (Martin-Merino et al., 2009).

USEFUL ORGANISATIONS

Samaritans

Samaritans is an organisation that allows you to share your problems with a volunteer off the record. Your conversation will remain confidential, and you can feel secure in expressing what is really troubling you. Making contact with someone from Samaritans is easy and can be done via phone, email, text, letter, or face-to-face. You don't have to be suicidal to ask for help. You may just want a friendly voice on the other end of the line to remind you that everyone has bad days and that bad days do not define you.

Papyrus

Papyrus is a national charity that aims to prevent young suicide. They believe that with the right support and education, many young suicides can be prevented. This is evident in their campaigns and endeavours to save young lives. Papyrus provides awareness and prevention training in order to prepare others with the knowledge and tools that can help prevent a suicide. In addition, the organisation provides confidential support and suicide intervention through HOPELineUK. And it empowers young people to lead suicide prevention activities in their own communities.

Mental Health Foundation

The Mental Health Foundation has a vast amount of information on different topics surrounding mental health for young people, both men and women. Their online website provides a range of statistics that paint a clear picture of what mental illness is like in reality, and how many people actually suffer from mental health problems. If you think that you might be suffering from some form of mental illness, the Mental Health Foundation lets you know that you're not alone.

Bibliography

Bromley, C., et al., *The Scottish Health Survey*, 2013 edition, vol. 1 (Edinburgh, 2014), http://www.gov.scot/Resource/0046/00464858.pdf (accessed 16 January 2017).

Fineberg, N., Haddad, P., Carpenter, L., Gannon, B., Sharpe, R., Young, A., Joyce, E., Rowe, J., Wellsted, D., Nutt, D. and Sahakian, B., 'The size, burden and cost of disorders of the brain in the UK', (*Journal of Psychopharmacology*, 2013 27(9)), 761–70.

Kessler, R. C., Berglund, P., Demler, O., Jin, R., Merikangas, K. R., Walters, E. E., 'Lifetime Prevalence and Age-of-Onset Distributions of DSM-IV Disorders in the National Comorbidity Survey Replication' (*Archives of General Psychiatry*, 2005, 62 (6)) 593–602. doi:10.1001/archpsyc.62.6.593.

Martin-Merino, E., Ruigomez, A., Wallander, M., Johansson, S., and Garcia-Rodriguez, L., 'Prevalence, incidence, morbidity and treatment patterns in a cohort of patients diagnosed with anxiety in UK primary care' (*Family Practice*, 2009 27(1)), 9–16.

McManus S, Bebbington P, Jenkins R, Brugha T. (eds.), 'Mental health and well-being in England' (*Adult Psychiatric Morbidity Survey 2014*. Leeds, 2016) http://content.digital.nhs.uk/catalogue/PUB21748/apms-2014-full-rpt.pdf (accessed 16 January 2017).

Mental Health Foundation, 'Statistics' https://www.mentalhealth.org.uk/statistics (accessed 16 January 2017).

Papyrus, 'About us', https://www.papyrus-uk.org/about (accessed 16 January 2017).

Samaritans, 'What happens when you contact us' http://www.samaritans.org/how-we-can-help-you/what-happens-when-you-contact-us (accessed 16 January 2017).

WHO, 'Caring for children and adolescents with mental disorders' (WHO, Geneva, 2003) http://www.who.int/mental_health/media/en/785.pdf [(accessed 16 January 2017).

Employment and Education

Employment

Everyone, especially young people, should be aware of their basic statutory rights where they are employed. Statutory rights are legal rights based on laws passed by Parliament, and your contract of employment is not allowed to take away any rights that you have by law.

Statutory Rights

Unless you are in a group of workers that are not entitled to some of these rights, for example freelance workers and those who are self-employed, then your statutory rights at work are as follows:

- The right to a written statement of terms of employment within two months of starting work.

- The right to an itemised pay slip. This applies from the day the employee starts work.

- The right to be paid the national minimum wage. This applies from the day the employee starts work.

- The right to not have illegal deductions made from pay. This applies from the day the employee starts work.

- The right to paid holiday. Full-time employees are entitled to at least twenty-eight days a year. Part-time employees are entitled to a pro rata amount.

- The right to time off for trade union duties and activities. This applies from the day the employee starts work. The time off doesn't have to be paid. Employees also have the right to be accompanied by a trade union representative to a disciplinary or grievance hearing. If an employee takes part in official industrial action and is dismissed as a result, this will automatically be an unfair dismissal.

- The right to paid time off to look for work if being made redundant. This applies once the employee has worked for two years for that employer.

- The right to time off for study or training for 16- and 17-year-olds. This applies from the day the employee starts work.

- The right to paid maternity leave.

- The right to paid paternity leave.

- The right to ask for flexible working.

- The right to take unpaid parental leave for both men and women.

- The right under health and safety law to work a maximum 48-hour working week. This applies from the day the employee starts work.

- The right under Health and Safety law to weekly and daily rest breaks. This applies from the day the employee starts work.

- The right not to be discriminated against. This applies from the day the employee starts work.

- The right to carry on working until you are at least 65.

- The right to notice of dismissal, provided you have worked for your employer for at least one calendar month.

- The right to written reasons for dismissal from your employer, provided you have worked for your employer for one year if you started before 6 April 2012, or two years if you started on or after that date.

- The right to claim compensation if unfairly dismissed. In most cases, to be able to claim unfair dismissal, you will have to have worked for your employer for one year if you started before 6 April 2012 or two years if you started on or after that date.

- The right to claim redundancy pay if made redundant. In most cases you will have had to have worked for two years to be able to claim.

- The right not to suffer detriment or dismissal for 'blowing the whistle' on a matter of public concern at the workplace. This applies from the day the employee starts work.

For more information or advice on your statutory rights at work, you can visit an experienced adviser at a Citizens Advice Bureau, who can assist you with concerns you may have about the workplace. I have used my local Citizens Advice Bureau to get advice on various matters to do with my business and my previous workplace. It is a free resource that is there to support you with legal matters and show you the right direction where possible.

Source

Citizens Advice Bureau, "Basic rights at work" https://www.citizensadvice.org.uk/work/rights-at-work/basic-rights-and-contracts/basic-rights-at-work/#h-rights-at-work (accessed 16 January 2017).

Education

If I had a penny for every time that fellow students have said that they felt like they needed to go to university in order to be qualified for a good job, I would be a wealthy young woman. It is believed that having a degree is the best way to open doors in the world of employment, but this has changed over time. A decade ago, someone with a good degree was more of a rarity compared to how many people are able to get a good degree today. Many people who have gone to university and left with a degree in a particular field are not working in that field. There is a shortage of jobs, and no matter how educated you are, if there are no jobs available in your field, then it is likely that you will end up working in a different area than you initially intended.

Attending university is not the only way to acquire knowledge and training in preparation for the workplace. There are alternative educational options that many people look down upon because it has been instilled in our minds that university is the dominant educational institution and the best educational direction.

APPRENTICESHIPS

Apprenticeships combine practical training in a job with study and can be a great way to gain experience whilst learning at the same time. Employers value experience and are more likely to choose the applicant that has experience in the role that they are applying for over the applicant that has a degree related to the role in question. This is because the applicant with the experience will take less time to train in the practical areas of the job role, which will save the employer money. Apprenticeships are available in various fields from construction to plumbing, and have equivalent educational levels (GOV, 2016):

- Intermediate – Level 2 – equivalent to 5 GCSE passes at grades A to C

- Advanced – Level 3 – equivalent to 2 A-level passes

- Higher – Levels 4, 5, 6 and 7 – equivalent to a foundation degree above

- Degree – Level 6 and 7 – equivalent to a bachelor's or master's degree

You shouldn't feel any less intelligent if you choose to opt for an apprenticeship instead of going to university. The equivalent educational levels should show you that even though you haven't attended university, you can still be educated at university level through an apprenticeship whilst getting valuable experience at the same time.

DISTANCE LEARNING

Distance learning is a way of learning remotely without being in regular face-to-face contact with a teacher in the classroom. At undergraduate level, distance learning involves students engaging with learning materials at home or work (The Complete University Guide, 2016). These materials are usually produced by the university or learning provider and are either sent to the student or accessed via the internet. Tutorial support is provided via a virtual learning environment set up by the university or learning provider, email, telephone, or other electronic means (Guide, 2016). The majority of UK undergraduate students study with the Open University, but many universities and other educational institutions offer distance learning programmes.

Advantages of distance learning include setting your own pace of study and having more control over your study (Guide, 2016). For example, it is your decision as to where and when you study, giving you more room for flexibility. The best thing about distance learning is that it often costs less than a full-time degree. The tuition fees for university, since being increased to £9,000 a year, is a significant deterrent to people interested in studying.

Distance learning allows you to get the same quality education whilst taking a different and more affordable approach to studying. On the other hand, the main disadvantage of distance learning is that you spend much of your time alone rather than surrounded by fellow students (Guide, 2016). This could lead to feelings of isolation and loneliness. It would be beneficial to vary the way you study so that you're not always studying on your own. For example, you could alternate between studying at home and studying at the library where you are able to interact with others that may also be studying.

SHORT COURSES

Short courses are a great way to expand your knowledge of subjects in a short period of time. There is a range of subjects to choose from in several industries, including fashion and technology. Short courses are practical because they are more affordable than studying at university and don't require long-term commitment.

Courses differ in duration. For example, one time you may do a marketing course that runs over seven days. Another time you may do a language course that runs over fourteen days. There are also short courses that can take up to one year to complete and that offer specifications on a certain topic or training to pass exams.

Short courses are available at educational institutions such as colleges and universities, but you can also find some short courses that are run by other learning centres. You don't have to limit yourself to studying in the UK, either. Educational institutions abroad offer short courses in different fields. An advantage of this is that these short courses are likely to be more affordable than studying in the UK. However, even though the short courses may be more affordable, if you are considering studying abroad for any length of time, it is important to take into account your expenses, e.g. how much it would cost to live abroad for the duration of your course and how you will get around safely.

SOURCES

- Gov.UK, 'Become an apprentice'(2016) https://www.gov.uk/apprenticeships-guide/overview (accessed 16 January 2017).

- The Complete University Guide, 'Why choose distance learning?' (2016) http://www.thecompleteuniversityguide.co.uk/distance-learning/advantages-and-disadvantages-%E2%80%93-why-choose-distance-learning/ (accessed 16 January 2017).

Funding

The Prince's Trust

The Prince's Trust is an established organisation that is always seeking out new ways to support young people through their work and research. They have eight core programmes that help young people from ages 13 to 30 to gain skills for the workplace through short vocational courses and personal development courses. Their Development Awards programme consists of cash awards for 14- to 25-year-olds to support getting back into work or training, and their Enterprise programme helps young people aged 18 to 30 with support and funding to work out if their business ideas are viable and if self-employment is the right for them. The Prince's Trust is a great place to start if you want some form of direction to go in when thinking about your career path and future.

https://www.princes-trust.org.uk

STARTUPS

Startups is an online resource that is the UK's number one service for starting a business. Not only does it provide tons of information on the dos and don'ts to consider when setting up a business, but it has multiple articles that are based on raising finance for your business idea. It is very difficult to find small business grants when doing research into funding opportunities, but Startups has compiled all this information together in one place, giving you everything you need to draw up a plan on how you want to go about setting up your business. They also give you an insight into how a business loan might be a viable option for some people and how the process of dealing with a business loan works.

http://startups.co.uk/small-business-grants/

ARTS COUNCIL ENGLAND

Quite a few organisations fund creative ideas and projects. The Arts Council England is just one of these. They have a funding finder that can make searching for funding relevant to what you would like to do much easier and less time-consuming. Grants for the Arts is their open access funding programme for individuals, arts organizations, and other people who use the arts in their works. They offer awards from £1,000–£100,000, depending on what your work is. And they support a variety of arts-related activities such as dance, theatre, literature, music, and combined arts. Even if your application is unsuccessful, they provide support to show you how you can still move forward with your project through other means.

http://www.artscouncil.org.uk/funding/grants-arts

UNLTD

UnLtd is a funding organisation for social entrepreneurs that is extremely competitive. They have different awards for different stages of an entrepreneur's work or project, including their Do It Award and Grow It Award. Their Do It Award is for people that want to create social change and already have a plan set in motion to do so. This award provides funding and support to work on this plan and separate what works from what doesn't work.

Their Grow It Award is for people that have identified a social issue and are passionate about tackling this issue. If you have experience and are ambitious with what you want to achieve but lack the funds and support to grow your idea, then this is the award for you.

UnLtd can give out only a certain number of awards per year. As a result, many people's applications have been unsuccessful, including mine when I was seeking funding for my *Time Is Money* project. That doesn't mean you should give up. Try applying again, and if that doesn't work, then try applying to somewhere else. Don't let rejection turn into demotivation.

https://unltd.org.uk/path/

EDUCATION ENDOWMENT FOUNDATION

The Educational Endowment Foundation (EEF) seeks to improve the educational attainment of children and young people from disadvantaged backgrounds. The organisation funds the development and the evaluation of affordable and scalable projects, breaking the link between family income and educational achievement. They are dedicated to ensuring that children and young people from less fortunate backgrounds are able to tap into their full potential and discover talents that they can build on for the future.

Knowledge is the key to everything. You can never know too much, and the learning process should always be appreciated. Education has played a crucial part in my development, and I have loved all the educational opportunities that I have been able to experience. It is a wonderful feeling to know that there are organisations like EEF that prioritise education for children and young people because they are the future. Education is one of the best investments they could make.

https://educationendowmentfoundation.org.uk/our-work/projects/

UK Grants

UK Grants was established in 1999 and has been helping businesses thrive ever since. They have created a database that has all their information in one place, making it easier for you to find what business grants are available to you. Their extensive website provides information on the different types of grants that are available for businesses and start-ups. They have also done their research into other grants that can help with the growth and development of your business, for example, grants that help with Web design, SEO, legal advice, accountancy and more. Whether you are seeking funding for your business idea or you just want some information on your options, UK Grants is the perfect place to build up knowledge on what is best for you and your business.

http://www.ukgrants.org/available-grants/

Courtney Barnes

Courtney Barnes is a 21-year-old photographer from London who currently studies at the University of West England in Bristol. I discovered Courtney on social media and instantly connected with her as a person and as a creative. She is passionate about photography, and I was looking for nothing less when I decided that I wanted images to accompany my writing for this book. Two years ago, Courtney decided to move three hours away from home and from everyone that she knew to start a new chapter in her life. She has expressed that it has been the best decision of her life so far. Her biggest motivation for pursuing photography was the idea of being able to create images that are true to the ideas that she has in her mind. She always found it frustrating to have ideas and concepts in her mind that she couldn't bring to life due to her lack of technical skill. She wasn't good at drawing and hadn't picked up a paintbrush since school, so she turned her attention to the one thing she knew she could commit to: photography.

Courtney is directly inspired by music, dance, and the people that surround her. She is interested in all elements of the arts. Her friendship group is made up of art and media creatives and social studies students. When I approached Courtney about taking the photographs for *Time Is Money*, she was excited to work on a project that was based around other creatives, especially the fashion designers of the team. Having her work published is something that Courtney has been aspiring to achieve for some time but just hasn't had the chance, so it makes me feel even better to know that I have helped her tick a goal off her list by giving her the opportunity to feature her work.

It is a common belief that if you're based in London, you prefer to work with people from London. Courtney has had her doubts about working from Bristol, believing that it has been a hindrance to her in some cases. However, in business, people who are serious about establishing working relationships with others will come to some arrangement about how that relationship will work. Business is all about give and take, and working with Courtney had nothing to do with how close or how far she was. It was based on her previous works and passion for what she did as a photographer. She hopes to work for both herself and a magazine publication in future, focusing particularly on fashion and her own concepts, with the aim of having an editorial fashion feature in the next two years.

Concluding Thoughts

All the themes and information provided in this book are interlinked and overlap in various ways. I have expressed the experiences that feature in *Time Is Money* in order to highlight that everyone, even those who are already on the path to success, has struggles and things that they can improve on. We have made mistakes, and we have taken risks. We have spent money to make money. Now we want to inspire others to do the same because making mistakes is a natural part of the growing process. Taking risks can take you to new heights that you didn't know exist. Saving is essential, but save to invest; don't save to save. Usually you have to spend money to make money, definitely so if you are a creative or a business person. Whatever you do, be it music, modelling, or writing, make a statement with it. Don't be afraid to make people remember you.

It wasn't easy for me to construct *Time Is Money*. Many creatives ignored me, both young and old. Many creatives gave me the runaround, pretending to be interested when they weren't. Some people put down my vision for *Time Is Money* completely, and I was okay with that. Those same people will remember me because I stuck at it. Despite their negativity I still wrote *Time Is Money* from a good place and learned a lot about people in the process.

It was attitudes like this that pushed me to let others know that not all people are unprofessional. Not all people will waste your valuable time that could have been used for something else. It was the people around me that displayed the negative energy towards me and what I was trying to do, but those people are no longer in my life. It is that easy to take control of your space. You know what you need to do to get to where you want to be, and this book gives you some of the basics to help get you started.

T K Williams-Nelson